Shut Up and Sell

Shut Up and Sell

✦

How to Say Less and Sell More

Craig Lawn

iUniverse, Inc.
New York Lincoln Shanghai

Shut Up and Sell
How to Say Less and Sell More

iUniverse, Inc.

For information address:
iUniverse, Inc.
2021 Pine Lake Road, Suite 100
Lincoln, NE 68512
www.iuniverse.com

Author's contact information:
Craig Lawn
POB 9398
Laguna Beach, CA 92652
craig@craiglawn.com
www.craiglawn.com

ISBN: 0-595-27517-6 (pbk)
ISBN: 0-595-65684-6 (cloth)

Printed in the United States of America

Contents

INTRODUCTION

Since 1947, the year I was born, the population of the world has more than tripled—a pretty significant change. The people inhabiting the earth have also changed significantly, becoming more sophisticated, street-smart and savvy about the merchandise and services available to them. Yet despite this fact—not to mention all the seminars, workshops and self-help books about sales and marketing available today—it's amazing how little the process of selling has changed over the past century. And there is no way that change can occur unless salespeople are willing to change themselves.

If you've bought this book, or if you're considering buying it, chances are you'd like to make more money selling, work more intelligently, feel more comfortable with your job, and sleep better at night. Well, for all that to occur, you're going to have to be willing to change—not your company, your boss, or your spouse—but yourself. That's the only thing you have full control over. You need to change yourself from the inside out, to step out of the box you're now in and begin to establish new practices you believe in, practices that will work.

If, as you read through this book, you come across a strategy, a technique, an approach or concept that you believe would help you sell more, it's time to change your usual way of selling. Not next week or tomorrow, but *now*. Follow this guideline and you will save time, make significantly more money, and come to enjoy more fully the process of selling.

1

NO CHANGE WITHOUT SELF-CHANGE

"It doesn't work to leap a twenty-foot chasm in two ten-foot jumps."

Over a hundred years ago, snake oil salesmen traveled around the country in wagons pulled by mules or horses. These salesmen had flashy clothes, gold watches, bed-rolls—and bottles of dyed water and extracts for sale. They sold their wares going from town to town, promising that their products would cure whatever ailed their customers. And they offered those willing to buy the first bottles the best deals in order to encourage quick sales.

The people who bought the first "cure-all" would tell the rest of the townspeople about the great product they'd found. It cured everything, they'd say, a bargain at twice the price—even though they didn't yet know if the "cure-all" would work. And if everyone bought in, those early buyers looked smart. After all, they'd been the first to act. Word would get around, and people would buy the product for a number of reasons: they were afraid to miss out on something valuable; they wanted to believe; they didn't want to feel left out; this might be the deal of a lifetime. In the end nobody was cured of anything; a lot of people had spent their money on something they neither wanted nor needed. And the snake-oil salesman had, of course, long since moved on—with their money—to the next town down the road.

Think this technique went out with the turn of the century? Think again. It's not just that the process of selling hasn't advanced much; in some ways it's even worse than it was in the snake oil days. What about the telemarketer who phones you while you're eating dinner—not to sell you anything, oh no, but only to tell you that you've won a prize and give you your claim number and a toll-free number to call to arrange for your free trip to San Diego, all expenses paid. Of course, when you call that number, you're told that all you have to do in exchange for your trip is listen to a ninety-minute presentation about a vacation club (read timeshare). Well, if free vacations are given away over the phone every night, why would anyone ever need to buy into a vacation club? Talk about snake oil. No wonder the timeshare business is doing so poorly today.

Or consider this scenario. You're invited to a dinner party in your neighborhood to introduce a new community going in at Lake Tahoe. Nothing is built yet, but there's going to be such a demand for the property that the company is going to have to sell it by lottery. All you have to do is put up a $5000.00 deposit, and in two months they'll fly you to Tahoe, where they'll draw names from a fishbowl and you'll get to choose your home site in the order the numbers are drawn. Supposing you're gullible enough to bite on this one, chances are your number will be one of the first picked, and for a huge price you can buy the lot of your choice, one of a kind, sure to go up in value two or three times in the next year. You leave for home having spent a huge amount of money—and a month later the salesperson calls again to let you in on the buy of a lifetime. Because you were smart enough to buy the first lot, you now have a chance to buy one in the next batch of lots *before* they go on sale to the general public. And already the lots have appreciated, so the one you paid $550,000 for is now worth $750,000, and it's even possible that you'll be allowed to buy two lots at that price. Well, how can you pass up a deal like that?

Word gets out and more people want their piece of the pie—a lot in a nice place where they can retire. And if they buy two, well, at the rate these lots are appreciating, this has to be the opportunity of a lifetime. Sound familiar? It happens all the time. The price of lots continues to soar even though very few people are actually building and living on the land. And somewhere a lot of people who were afraid of missing a great deal, didn't want to be left out, or thought they'd make a lot of money on re-sales, are stuck with some very expensive land that they can't sell for half what they paid for it. You get the picture—more snake oil. And this scene is played over and over again every day with all kinds of products, from water purifiers and air filters to vitamins and skin creams.

Salespeople are, for the most part, still relying on outdated techniques to attract buyers and sell products today, bombarding them with puffy ads containing claims that could not possibly be true. How many towns, for example, can really contain the #1 Toyota dealership in the country? How can more than one dealer make this claim? It's amazing that anyone still buys into this garbage. "We've sold more cars than any other dealer in Arizona." Who cares? In fact, do people really want to support someone who already has so much success he's bragging about it on TV and in magazines?

When I train sales staff in high-end residential and golf communities throughout the United States, I am constantly amazed by the silly shuck and jive tactics still used by salespeople who consider themselves to be both professional and sophisticated. How often have I heard someone suggest statements like these to get a buyer to sign a contract: "A lot of people are looking at that house. If you want it, you'd better buy it today." or "We're selling everything as soon as it becomes available...." It doesn't take a whole lot of intelligence to wonder why, if everything is selling so fast, the developer is paying salespeople hundreds of thousands of dollars a year to sell property that is being touted as selling itself.

Another common—and equally ineffective—technique is to pitch a product without giving a thought to the buyer's wants, needs, and proposed timetable. Some salespeople seem to think that if they simply keep talking and showing their wares, the customer will eventually buy just to shut them up. These snake oil approaches are becoming less viable as buyers become more sophisticated. Of course, those tactics never did work in the long run. That's why snake oil was sold from the back of a wagon. The salesmen never stayed anywhere for very long.

If you consider the way society has come to view most car dealers, who commonly refuse to tell customers the bottom line price for a car, instead badgering them to reveal what they are willing to spend—or those universally hated telemarketers who phone just as you're climbing into the bathtub or getting ready to sit down to dinner—you may well wonder why on earth outdated, ineffective sales approaches are still being used. The plain and simple fact is that potential customers want to be talked *with*, not talked *at;* they want to be told the truth, not shuck and jive. The easiest way today for you to separate yourself from the vast majority of salespeople, and to sell more in the process, is to learn to talk with your customers. In helping them to solve any problems they may have regarding the purchase of a product, you will be motivating them to buy. You cannot treat customers identically; no two are alike. But you must give them equal attention. Most buys are emotional. People buy what they want more often than what they need. And a salesperson can find out what customers want only by talking with them and listening carefully to what they say.

My question is this: why are we salespeople so reluctant to change our sales approaches? What makes us continue to think we can jam our products down our customers' throats? Are we so frightened of change that we can't step out of the boxes we are in, reevaluate our sales techniques, and try something different and more effective? The usual methods of selling in the United States today still have everything in common with those of the snake oil salesmen—even though most people making purchases say they are not happy with the behavior of the sales personnel involved. Would a change in the behavior of salespeople perhaps result in more sales? What do we have to lose? Why not try something new?

In my industry, the number of people who purchase a piece of real estate in a residential golf course community has dwindled to less than four percent of those who are shown property in such communities. That means more than ninety-six percent of our potential customers are not buying! And still most developers/managers of golf course communities feel they are doing their best, telling sales representatives simply to stick to sales fundamentals—whatever that means. Sure, someone may change a word or two in a sales pitch or coin a cute phrase here or there. Another may attempt a trial close or use a close-ended question or emotional tie-down. ("If I show you something you really like and you think it's a good value, you're going to buy something like that? Right?) Still others may even try to figure out a customer's personality type and then attempt to manipulate that customer into buying something he may not really want or need. The pitch may sound clever, but behind the fancy new window dressing, it's the same old snake oil routine. And for anyone who wants to sell more effectively, it's time to move on.

Instead of taking the same tired routine to a new place, you might consider an alternative: real change. All of us in sales would like to make more money with less effort and enjoy our jobs more in the process. But in order to accomplish these goals, we need to be willing to change, and change is usually accompanied by some degree of pain or sacrifice. What needs to change is not our location, the companies we work for, our bosses, our mates, even some of the basic sales procedures we have learned. We need to change the one thing we have any real control over: *ourselves*. And we have to change from the inside out—the way we feel, act, and respond to what is happening around us as we are working. Rather than relying on the way selling has always been done, we need to step out of the box and start looking for something we believe in, something that will work better. The most successful salespeople, the best producers, are doing just that. And their methods of selling are very different from those of their peers.

Consider an example from another field, professional golf. Tiger Woods was the youngest golfer ever to win the Masters—and by the most strokes ever. After his triumph in Augusta Georgia, one might have expected him to bask in his glory. If his methods had worked this time, why wouldn't he simply continue to use them? But that wasn't Tiger's way. Within hours of winning, he quietly stepped out of the box and began to work at changing his golf swing—not altering one or two aspects of it, but working on the entire swing: stance, grip, tempo, rotation, swing plane, mental preparation, everything. Why would he do this? Why, when everything seemed to be going splendidly, was he fixated on change? Because he had the vision and drive to look not at what had worked today, but at what might be needed to work in the future. He looked at his career in the long term. If he kept swinging like a man of twenty-one, he might find that as his body aged, he would one day no longer be able to make such fast, sweeping moves. Unlike the salesperson who relies on the idea of selling today as though there will be no tomorrow, Tiger Woods took a risk, a long-term approach that initially cost him. The following year was his worst ever as a professional. But he stuck to his new routine and over the next two years made golf history, breaking records that even the experts thought would never be broken.

So you aren't the Tiger Woods of your company? Maybe you're the number two or three sales producer? Or maybe you haven't even teed up yet, haven't sold before. In that case, you have even less to lose than a veteran salesperson. The point is, wherever you are in terms of sales, you can learn to do better, to sell the best *you* can by improving your selling game with techniques that will last long-term. You can learn not to go just for the quick sale, but for the one that creates a relationship with your customer, generating referrals, trust, and more sales—as well as a competitive edge. Learning to talk with and listen to your potential customers is a sales approach that will stand the test of time.

At this point I think it's important to understand fully the difference between your personal beliefs and your attitude toward the products you're selling. This may come as something of a shock, but it isn't necessary for you to believe in a product in order to be a really effective, straightforward, honest salesperson. What meets your aesthetic, emotional or financial needs has nothing to do with what meets those of your client.

Several years ago I was selling expensive real estate in a golf course community in Pawley's Island, South Carolina, when I suddenly realized that I didn't believe in the product I was selling. I was marketing it successfully—in fact, I was selling twice as much property as anyone else on the sales team. But I didn't *like* the community: rows of what I considered unattractive homes with buyers all trying to outdo one another in terms of ostentatious living. You know, the fulfillment of the American Dream. Most residents seem to think that working out involved a hard day of driving around the golf course in an electric cart while drinking beer, followed by happy hour at the clubhouse, where they argued about the proper length of grass in the rough or who had left a bike sitting in his front yard. "Oh my gosh," I thought, "am I turning into one of those salespeople who will sell anything to anyone just to make a buck?" I walked around for days not talking much to anyone, trying to figure out what I was turning into. I even wondered if I'd picked the wrong profession. Finally I had to present my case to the ultimate consultant, my wife. "Lisa," I said, "what is happening to me? I don't believe in what I'm selling. What kind of salesman am I? I think I'm turning into one of those shuck and jive types, selling just to sell."

Lisa's response surprised me. "Wrong, Craig—I think you're just the opposite. You believe in the customers and *their* wants and needs. After all, that's what's really important. You're not trying to sell people anything they don't want; in fact, you're selling them what they *do* want. It doesn't matter that you wouldn't want to live on that golf course; they do."

I thought about what Lisa was saying, and at first it sounded too simplistic; I felt she was only being supportive. But eventually her words began to make real sense, and now it seems to me that a mark of the very best salespeople is their ability to overlook what they might find distasteful and concentrate on the wants and needs of the customer, to look at every potential sale from the *buyer's* point of view. I now consider this to be the first rule of effective selling: ***Try to sell only to people who really want your product or services.*** Do this, and you'll sell more of whatever it is you're selling. You'll also save a good deal of time you're probably now wasting on customers who aren't interested in what you have to sell.

If your customer wants a pair of plaid pants, a purple car, or a house twenty feet from a highway, it's all right to sell it. It's the job of the salesperson not to make judgments about the product being sold, but to find out as precisely as possible what the customer wants and then try to find a match. What salespeople have to believe in is not the products they are selling, but the wishes of the customers they are selling those products to. Taking a personal interest in customers and finding out what it is they want is a technique that works. So don't worry about what others may think; just do what you think best for you and your customer.

If you think this sounds too easy, you're probably right. It isn't easy to change old patterns. Look at how difficult it is for smokers to give up their habits. The vast majority of them believe at some level that smoking is going to damage their health—even as they try to rationalize their behavior. Yet they continue to smoke. Why? Aside from the physical addiction, it's their habit; they have fallen into a routine, and they don't want to do what it takes to change. The simple fact is, all they have to do is *stop*. Stop and it's over—except, of course, the pain, the craving.

Fortunately, there is no physical addiction to complicate the changing of one's sales techniques, but there are still similarities. Change is easy to believe in and easy to talk about; however, carrying it out is quite another thing. It's not hard to find a salesman who can *talk* about honesty and trust, putting the customer first, listening, and providing the best customer service possible. Yet you would be hard pressed to find many salespeople who are *practicing* these qualities in their efforts to sell. Change is difficult. But with discipline and courage, old habits can be replaced by new, better habits with happier and healthier results. Consider the fact that really effective salespeople are among the highest paid individuals on the planet today.

When to make a change once you've bought into a concept or approach? The only time to change is *now*. Seize the moment. Don't give your mind the chance to start rationalizing by saying next week, tomorrow, even in an hour. Change *now*. Stop the old habits and you've stopped. Start a new routine and you've started. To paraphrase and embellish what the Buddha said, live your personal life as though each moment is your last—and handle your business as though it will last forever.

NOTES

2

NO DUMPING ALLOWED

✦

(or That's a Little More Information Than I Need to Hear…).

○ ○
"Well-timed silence hath more eloquence than speech."

Without question, the easiest sales technique, and the one with the most immediate results for any salesperson who wants to start selling more, is to start talking less. In other words, shut up and sell! Do less than fifty percent of the talking and guess what? If you start listening to potential buyers, you'll start selling a lot more effectively. Potential buyers and customers want to be talked *with*, not talked *at*. Do less than fifty percent of the talking, and you have an opportunity to gain the trust and respect of your prospect. You will also separate yourself from the ninety-five percent of salespeople whose practice is to dump information, and you will sell more than you are currently selling. Whether you deal in ear-rings wholesale for a dollar a pair or homes worth millions of dollars, there is no need to overwhelm prospective customers by telling everything you know about your product in the first few minutes of meeting them. Great salespeople must certainly have extensive knowledge about their products or services; they must also have the wisdom to know when—or if—they should deliver it.

In today's environment consumers are offered a huge range of choices, and the purchases they make are usually based on their emotional response to the products offered. It is desire, not need or any manipulative tactic a salesperson might make, that drives sales. A customer may have a per-ceived need, but the ultimate decision comes from the emo-tions. After all, do any of us really *need* new cars, new homes, three baths, six-disk changers, air-conditioning, two carat rings, private schools for our children, new computers, or even new clothes? And if sales are based on a customer's emotional response, what is the purpose of dumping a lot of information before getting some idea of what it is that cus-tomer really wants?

Consider this scenario, a dialogue between a particularly ineffective salesperson and a prospective buyer:

Salesperson: "Welcome to Paradise Plantation, a community where everyone is happy and is treated like family."

Prospective Buyer: *Well, I don't know about your family, but hearing this doesn't make me want to buy.* Silence.

Salesperson: "How did you hear about us? Ad in the newspaper? Radio, TV, friend, real estate agent? What brings you to Paradise—the Plantation, that is?"

Prospective Buyer: "Saw the sign. Just happened to be in the neighborhood." *Yeah, right. We live in Chicago. We got on a plane, rented a car, checked into a hotel nearby, and now we just happen to be driving past.*

Salesperson: "Well, we're happy to have you here. Let me tell you a little bit about our community."

Prospective Buyer: "Okay. Sure."

Salesperson: "Joe Schmoe, who developed Paradise Plantation, was a real visionary. We see it as the most unique community of its kind in the entire country. The clubhouse is a 37,000 square foot building three stories high, built partially from 160,000 hand-made bricks. It has two-hundred-year-old doors that Mr. Schmoe and his wife brought back from a castle they found during their trip to France a couple of years ago, and it contains a fully-stocked pro-shop, private and public dining areas, men's and women's locker rooms, a men's grill and bar, a grill room for both sexes, meeting rooms, a formal dining room, a bar, a private dining room for members only, a card room, a comfortable lobby for conversing with family and friends, eleven fire places, a recreational center with ping-pong, three pool tables and all sorts of nifty games, a cart barn for our golf carts, a state-of-the-art kitchen, a Wall Street room complete with ticker tape and CNN business news 24/7, the all-important internet room with five of the latest color Macintosh iMacs connected to our fiber optic cable that runs throughout the entire community—more than twenty-seven miles of fiber cable, I might add—a library with the latest best sellers as well as the classics, a fully-equipped craft room with lessons every other Tuesday and Thursday evenings, a state-of-the-art driving range with free balls for members, two eighteen-hole world-class championship golf courses designed by the best golfers in the world with bent grass greens and Bermuda Tipton #39 fairways—a hybrid especially grown for our climate—with 18,000 electronic sprinkler heads, 112 sand traps, six tee boxes to choose from (so our course is just perfect for either the beginner or the pro golfer), a slope rating of 128, three tier sewers and watershed, twenty-four hour security guard, 852 home sites, trees, 127 golf villas, state-of-the art-fitness center, the finest equestrian center in the country with stalls for forty-two horses, a 35,000 square foot indoor arena, two full-time trainers (and, of course, the entire facility is climate controlled so your horse won't get a sniffle), 652 acres of common or green area, seven miles of walking and jogging paths, a spa and fitness center complete with Nautilus equipment, stair-master, free-runner, elliptical trainer, fourteen TVs for your viewing pleasure while working out, full-time attendant, personal trainers, two massage rooms, seven showers, a steam room, sauna, whirlpool, two swimming pools, one for laps and one for family swimming, an aerobic room offering classes three times a week during the evenings and four times a week during the day, a nursery for your kids, six tennis courts—four hard true and two composition, three of them lighted for night play—a movie theater that shows first run movies two nights a week, a convenience store open seven days a week and, of course, a one-half scale train with a full-time engineer so your kids can enjoy riding throughout the entire property. Now we offer homes ranging from 1200 to 5500 square feet, villas from 900 to 3700 square feet, casitas from 1500 to 4600 square feet, lots from one-third of an acre to two and one-half acres, and we can set you up with quarter-share, half-share, fractional time-share and vacation club. Any questions?"

Prospective Buyer: "How much do the homes here run?"

Saleperson: "One to five million."

Prospective Buyer: "Oh, we couldn't possibly afford that. We'd have to win the lottery. Guess we're out."

Salesperson: "Perhaps you might consider looking at this as an investment. Consider the value."

A little late for the value pitch, wouldn't you say? Sorry, but I think that seller lost those clients somewhere between the 160,000 hand-made bricks it took to build the club-house and the twenty-seven miles of fiber optic cable.

Think this scenario sounds like an exaggeration? It's a slightly overdrawn representation of actual initial presentations I've heard over the last several years at golf course and new home communities. In most of these presentations the salesperson does ninety-five percent of the talking and the customer five. And the only time the salesperson is really listening during that five percent is the moment the credit card number is given.

Surely you wouldn't try this kind of approach at home. If you did, you might soon be looking for a new home as well as a new relationship. Let me give you a more personal example of the importance of shutting up in order to sell. A few years ago my wife and I moved to a small town in northern California, and we had trouble finding a home that was suitable to our needs—or should I say our wants. We searched for over a year. One afternoon I met a man at work who said he had a carriage house with a stable that he was going to put on the market in the next couple of days. He asked if I would like to take a look at it, so I checked it out by myself and discovered that the carriage house had a small apartment above it where we could live while we converted the bottom floor into our dream house. *How quaint*, I thought, *over five acres for our dogs and pet rabbit, a stable for any horses we might buy in the future. And the asking price is fantastic. Great views. Awesome...I have to have it!*

At this point I had to make a decision. Was I going to practice what I preach? Or would I just go home to Lisa and start dumping information about how great the view was, the potential, the fabulous price, the value I perceived, the fun I would have living there? I wondered if Lisa would see this place the same way I did. Probably not—at least not exactly. Did you ever tell someone about something with so much excitement and passion that when they finally saw what you were talking about, they were disappointed? Well, that's what I was afraid to do with Lisa: dump information and kill the deal. So I decided to tell her only a little about the place, introduce her to the idea in the most objective way I could. I wanted her to see it at once but, of course, that was up to her.

When I got home and we'd settled down with a glass of wine to talk, I said, "Lisa, I just saw a property I really liked. It's a carriage house with an apartment above it, and it overlooks a small village in the valley. It has a horse stable, a fence around the yard. It would need a lot of work to make it the way we want, but it has potential."

Lisa's response was excruciatingly casual. "Sounds nice. Maybe we can look at it together next week."

What next week? I thought. *It will be gone.* I wanted to insist that we go right then to look at it, but I managed to control my emotions. "Lisa, I'd like you to look at it as soon as you can because it goes on the market in a couple of days, and I think it will sell immediately. We'll probably lose the opportunity to buy it if we wait until next week. Your opinion is important to me and I want to know how you feel about it."

Lisa immediately responded to my request. "Let's look at it tonight," she said.

Thank goodness I kept my mouth shut enough that I didn't get in the way of what Lisa wanted, how she felt about this place for herself and for us. I am happy to report it was what we both wanted. We bought it that very night, started fixing it up right away, and we've lived in it for over four years. We love it.

I didn't have to sell Lisa on the house—I just let her look at it and decide for herself whether or not it met her needs and wants. And my approach with her translates over into sales of any kind. All customers are going to want to know what's in it for them, so when a salesperson who has just been waiting for the next victim to come in starts dumping information, the potential customer takes a defensive posture. And what does the bad salesperson do if the customer doesn't buy? Blame it on the customer, of course—he was a tire kicker, a looky-lou, a liar (after all, aren't all buyers liars, saying they can't afford the merchandise?), a geek. The list goes on and on. What these salespeople never seem to consider is that all those losers go to another salesperson with more expertise and buy. All potential customers, especially in America, eventually buy something—tire kickers, liars, and geeks included. And they usually buy from someone who figured out what they wanted, solved some problem, and provided a product or service that worked for them.

If you want to become more effective at selling, it would be prudent to take a hard look at the amount of dumping most of your counterparts are doing and see an opportunity to separate yourself from the pack. There is no greater or faster way to distinguish yourself as a salesperson and gain rapport and trust with customers than to separate yourself from the stereotype salesperson. And all you have to do is *listen* to the people you are trying to sell to. Identify a problem or a want and see if you have a solution for it. No solution? Thank them, send them on their way, and move forward.

Not only should we shut up and listen to what the prospect has to say; we also need to come up with probing questions that get potential customers to start talking about themselves and what they want. Whenever you enter a store, a salesperson immediately asks, "Can I help you?" And what do you think is the most common response to this question? Right, the one you always use yourself: "No thanks, just looking," the customer's first line of defense. Now if the first word out of the mouths of most potential customers is "*No,*" why is it that salespeople continue to use the same old line? And why start out by putting the burden on the customer? It might seem a small detail at this point in the relationship, but there's never a second chance for a first impression. What about something like this: "I don't know whether or not I can help you with anything, but if you find something you like, let me know and I'll be happy answer any questions you might have."

I recently walked into a Banana Republic while I was on a business trip in Arizona. I needed a pair of socks for an upcoming sales seminar I was giving. The salesperson politely asked if she could help me. Almost automatically I said, "No thanks, just looking." Actually I know where the socks are in every Banana Republic in the country—right near the cash register so you can buy them while you're waiting in line to pay for something else. And saying that I was "just looking" made me feel a little uncomfortable. I wasn't just looking. I was looking specifically for a pair of socks, but I didn't want a stranger helping me pick them out. I went directly to the sock rack, where the socks are neatly displayed on little hangers, wondering vaguely if anyone really has a tiny rack in a closet on which to hang socks. As I took a couple of pairs off the rack, a cold feeling shot down my spine, the feeling that someone was stalking me. Yes, someone was. The salesclerk was standing about one foot behind me, watching me maneuver my way through the tiny sock hangers in search of the right socks to wear to my seminar. I gave a glance back, hoping the woman was intuitive enough to see that I was asking for more space and a little privacy. *Yes, you can help me. Get out of here and leave me alone,* I wanted to say. Having given her my best get-out-of-my-face stare, I was stunned by her next remark. "If you'd like to try something on, there are dressing rooms in the back."

I had to ask. Wouldn't you? "Do people actually try on socks?"

"No."

"Then why did you suggest that to me. I'm just curious."

"Well, I felt uncomfortable not saying anything, and I didn't know what to say, so I just said that."

Her candor left me wondering. It's sometimes not a fancy sales trick but just a salesperson's discomfort that leads to inane remarks. Some people simply can't handle silence. And that led to more conversation. "I'm out in Arizona to work with a company's sales force to teach them techniques for selling their products more effectively," I told her. "Could you tell me, has your company offered you any training?"

"Yes," she said, "they have a two-week course that's required for everyone who's going to be selling out front."

"And what do they teach you?" I asked.

"Beside teaching us company procedures and how to operate the computer, they give us ways to treat the customer."

"Mind sharing?" I asked.

"No."

"What do they say to do when the customer walks in the door?"

"Just greet them."

"Did they tell you to ask the customer if you could help?" I was keeping the conversation friendly, being my charming self as I probed away.

"They said we shouldn't ask if we can help. It puts the burden on the customer. They said we should look ready to serve, just be available and not follow the customer around the store. Just be ready."

"Hey," I said, "no offense, I'm just asking, but why did you ask me if you could help?" I should have been able to predict her response.

"It just felt funny not saying anything but hello."

This difficulty with keeping quiet is a pretty typical trait, common to some degree with salespeople no matter where you meet them—looking for new home, a car, a pair of shoes, or just looking. Despite what training salespeople may be given, their presentations are usually developed around their own comfort levels and insecurities, not directed to the customer's needs or desires. In that process lies the greatest mistake a salesperson can make: filling any moment of potential silence with stuff that doesn't need to be said in a misguided effort to look and feel knowledgeable. Not much wisdom in that technique.

When the question "Can I help you?" is asked, a reasonable response might go as follows: "Yes, could you please tell me a little about your store? I've never been in one before, and I'm not sure exactly how it works. If I find something I like, do I just take it home, or is there a procedure I need to follow?" You get the picture.

The truth is, people will buy more merchandise more frequently if they are given the freedom to set their own agendas. In this day of almost unlimited choices and sophisticated buyers, salespeople need to be ready to serve, to answer questions, and to ask tactful questions that may get the prospect to open up. Then they will have the knowledge necessary to find the right product for that person. This approach means no sale in some cases, but that's okay. Also, if you're starting your presentation with the word *I*, you might want to rethink the way you start it. Isn't the customer supposed to be number one? Put the customer first, and you will make more sales.

The words *just looking* are only a defense. They mean, "Give me space. Let me get familiar with your place of business, your product or services or you. Let me get comfortable, and then maybe we'll talk. But for now just leave me alone, please." Sixty-six percent of the people who walk into a Banana Republic and say they're just looking end up buying something. In their case does "just looking" really mean "just buying"? What does it mean for *your* business, product or services?

So how does a salesperson get customers to open up, say what they're really looking for, what they want? Well, it depends. (A consultant's two favorite words.) But it *does* depend—on a lot of different factors. Waiting on tables? It's reasonable to assume that your customers have come to eat, to drink, or both. Always true? Probably not, but certainly true most of the time. Selling real estate? Should the assumption be that the prospect who comes to your office does so in order to purchase a piece of property? Probably, but not always. The major difference between these two types of sales is the time it takes to complete the sales process. It might take anywhere from half an hour to three hours to have drinks and/or a meal, but probably a month to several years to make a large purchase such as a home or a piece of commercial real estate. Still, a sale is a sale, and refraining from dumping information will work equally well for both types.

For example, let's say you walk into a restaurant. What is it that you want first? Bet you answered, "It depends." (Didn't know you were a consultant, did you?) It depends on who you are, the mood you are in, the amount of time you have available for the meal, the time of day, etc. For the server (our salesperson in this case) to sell effectively, he or she needs to find out what you want and then use that knowledge to provide the best service possible. Saying please and thank you and rattling off a long list of specials, giving a detailed description of how each one is prepared (dumping information) won't cut it. Might as well say to you, "I'm going to tell you all about our specials tonight. I don't care if you want a drink right now or if you don't particularly want to hear them; I'm going to tell you about them anyway. Then there's the menu. Everything on it is good, everyone who comes here loves everything, and our chef always makes everything perfectly." Wow! What a way to start off a relationship, to gain rapport and trust. And just to make this approach even less appealing, let's say that your spouse, who is with you, is a vegetarian. The long discourse on four different ways the chef prepares dead cow is certainly not going to do anything to build trust with her.

Let me cut to the chase and give you an example of a great opening I experienced at a restaurant in Scottsdale, Arizona during my trip there. I sat down at an outside table, and within moments a waitress came up to me and asked, "Is there anything you would like to have happen real fast?" I said, "Yes, a glass of wine, red, cab, Sterling. Thanks." I got my wine immediately. After that, listening to the list of specials (which I always suspect to be composed of what didn't sell the night before) didn't seem nearly so irritating.

What happened here is that the waitress gave me an opportunity to set my own agenda with an open-ended question: She asked me what *I* wanted. She didn't consider what she wanted or her boss might want; she didn't try to impose her agenda on me or manipulate me. What a great start—and, I might add, as a finish she got a great tip. I was talked *with*, not *at*. Salespeople who use this approach are more effective, have happier clients, and are happier themselves. Also, they sell more. When a customer opens up, the person selling has an opportunity to hear exactly what is wanted in terms of a particular product or service. And once a salesperson has that knowledge, the strategy of how to sell—what to demonstrate, what to say, and what not to say—becomes quite clear.

The open-ended question is the number one way to get a customer to open up. This is a question that cannot be answered with one word, a *yes* or *no*. Try questions like these: "If you could live in any community you wanted to, describe the one you'd pick"; "What would you expect the ideal sales trainer to teach your sales force?" "What process does your company follow when adding a new product like X, Y, or Z to their store?" And, of course, "What would you like to have happen real fast today?" Notice anything these questions have in common? Open-ended questions start with words such as *What? How? When? Where?*

Open-ended questions get the prospect to think, and that's something the potential customer is rarely asked to do by salespeople today. By asking open-ended questions, you are asking for your client's opinions, showing that those opinions are important, making the client a part of the process. And you get the information you need to make a good presentation. There is no subject prospects enjoy more than talking about themselves, but most salespeople are afraid to ask open-ended questions. They're afraid of the answers the prospect might give, worried about a possible rejection. These salespeople apparently figure that if they do most of the talking, customers will not have a chance to reject them and will eventually get so worn out that they will buy the product just to get out the door. Right? Wrong. Nothing could be further from the truth.

Today's sophisticated buyer is demanding more and more in the way of consultation. No tricks, just conversation, open-ended questions and an honest representation of the product or services. Guess what? Three times out of four, people buy because they trust the salesperson and believe he is telling the truth. Trust is the number one reason people decide to buy—not price, not product, not a friendly salesperson. Whether we're talking about a bracelet or a boat, honesty and sincerity come ahead of friendliness when customers talk about their reasons for buying. (Friendliness finished a distant third in two recent surveys.) Also remember that it's the second or third sale, not the first, where salespeople make their money, either from repeat business or referrals. The pros aren't after one quick sale; they're in it for the long run. If you're in it for the short term, you'll probably have a short career.

So now maybe you think you're ready to start trying out open-ended questions on your next prospect. Sounds easy enough, you think? Well, the technique is easy to talk about, but it can be difficult to do, at least until you get into the habit of doing it—particularly if you have already established the bad sales habit of asking close-ended questions. Do you prefer this model home or that one? Would you like to meet on Tuesday or Wednesday? (Logical response to that one? "Well, actually I would like to meet on Monday, but since that wasn't an option, let's just not meet.") Close-ended question close people down. They leave no room for the prospect to think, only to choose within the limits of your questions. So when you ask a potential customer an open-ended question, the first thing you will hear is silence. That's a rare sound in today's selling environment, but it's the sound of the customer thinking over the question and formulating a response. Those three to six seconds—or more—of silence can be scary to the salesperson trying this technique for the first time. There's an immediate temptation to say something to fill the space, to ask a quick yes or no question.

For example, suppose you just asked your customer, "If you could have any home you wanted, what would you be looking for?" Silence.... More silence. Don't jump in with several more questions—"Two bedrooms? Two baths? One story?" This is known as machine gunning, asking a customer question after question without being considerate enough to wait for an answer to any of them. Not only is this technique irritating to people, it's downright rude. Just ask the open-ended question and then *shut up*. Listen to the sound of the customer thinking. Wait while those seconds pass. Count them if you want to. (*One thousand one, one thousand two....*) It may seem forever before you get an answer, and the silence will feel awkward. But most change does. And remember, there will be no change in your effectiveness in sales unless you're willing to change yourself.

There's also what is called the open-ended command. Sometimes as a customer is beginning to open up, telling you what he honestly wants, he'll suddenly begin to feel vulnerable and start holding back. At this point a good salesperson may be able to use an open-ended command to get the customer talking again. Here are some examples: "Tell me more"; "Keep going"; "Could you explain that in a little more detail?"

Salespeople from around the country who have attended my sales seminars tell me that the single best tool they've learned from these seminars is to ask open-ended questions instead of dumping information. These people have learned to shut up and sell.

NOTES

3

THEY COME WITH THEIR DUKES UP

✦

(And Can You Blame Them?)

When a potential buyer walks into a place of business, no matter whether it's a restaurant, a retail store, a wholesale outlet, or a resort real estate community, the biggest thing on that customer's mind is, "What's in it for me?" Customers enter any place of business with their dukes up. They want to protect themselves, and do you blame them? They know very well that the first thing on the salesperson's mind is what's in it for *him*. The prospective buyer thinks, "If I buy something from this salesperson, I know I will benefit him, his family and his boss, but will whatever I buy benefit *me*? Will it be something I really want and can use? I don't care in the least what this waiter's favorite meal is (or this salesperson's favorite house plan in the subdivision, or the piece of jewelry that clerk finds most beautiful). I know the 'favorite' item is likely to be the one that will bring in the biggest tip, the fattest commission, or the highest bonus in the shortest possible time. I know all about those bonuses that companies put on their least desirable merchandise so salespeople will push hard to sell it to people who don't really want it—while the good stuff sells itself."

It's no wonder that today's sophisticated customers come into a place of business with a protective wall around themselves. Salespeople have one of the worst collective reputations of any profession. And guess what? Most of them deserve it. What's your image of a typical salesperson? What was your last buying experience like? Chances are it involved a sales pitch coming from a fast-talking salesperson with high-pressure tactics: "this is one of a kind"; "this deal isn't going to be there tomorrow"; "a lot of other people are looking at that one, so you'd better not wait"; "this offer won't last long"; "that one looks great on you"; "prices are going up next week"; "this is the best deal in the city (state, country, world, universe)"; "you owe it to yourself"; "it's state-of-the-art, world-class, everyone's buying it"; "honestly, let me be frank with you, I wouldn't lie to you"; "it's guaranteed for life"; "you can't go wrong with this one"; "if you have any problem with it, you can just give me a call"; "thirty percent off, fifty percent off" (of what, nobody ever says). And the worst: "trust me." If that isn't a signal to look out, I don't know what is. It's no wonder prospects start out feeling emotionally defensive. How many times do you have to get hit before you start protecting yourself?

Of course this doesn't mean that *all* salespeople are deceptive or manipulative, but far too many are, and it is from them that the public has formed its perception. How can everyone represent the world's most unique community, best-selling car, best service? How many salespeople could honestly claim that every one of their customers is happy, never a complaint? And how often is a product in such short supply that it won't last long? So when potential customers come through a place of business and say, "just looking"; "not buying today"; "don't need any help, just a brochure if you have one"; "not in our budget, can't afford it"; "have to think about it"; "we'll give you a call"; "need to speak to our accountant, our kids, our business partners"; "yeah, it's great, get back to you," these are just defenses, ways customers use to protect themselves from all the abuse they and their friends and families have been subjected to all their lives by manipulative sales techniques that are certainly less than honest. It takes time to break down a customer's defenses and begin the process of building the rapport and trust necessary to sell effectively, but a good salesperson can speed up the process. And rapport and trust are necessary if a salesperson is to develop long-term and rewarding relationships with clients. Good salespeople are sincere, genuine, and empathetic; they listen to and respect their potential customers. Once a potential buyer does trust and respect a salesperson, that buyer becomes a great sales asset, sending referrals who will regard the salesperson as credible from the beginning. This is the result that most salespeople want, but only the good ones are getting.

A large part of the problem is that many salespeople have very little respect for their prospective buyers. When I ask salespeople to describe their potential customers, listing some of their characteristics and speculating on why most of them don't buy, here are some of the comments I hear: "They don't know what they want"; They're "bullshitters" or "indecisive engineer types who don't buy" or "not our type of customer." They "don't understand our product." And, of course, the salesperson's all-time classic, "buyers are liars." These salespeople are missing the point in their inability to understand that what a person says does not necessarily reveal his real intent. They fail to recognize the potential customer's defenses for what they are. Although it might be stretching it to say that a salesperson may be the direct cause of any individual prospect's behavior, the fact remains that these defenses exist, and the salesperson who is able to deal with the customer's fear or distrust directly will sell more of whatever he or she is selling. Find out what is behind these emotional walls, and you will probably find a sale. Certainly you will find more sales then you are finding now if you think of all your potential customers as geeks, tire kickers and liars.

Buyers are liars. True. But I say liars are buyers. Think about it. Everyone has bought something from someone at some time. Would Nordstrom refuse to sell to a liar? ("No, I'm sorry. You told me you were broke and couldn't afford that ring, and now you say that your parents will be paying for it. We have a strict policy here. Since you weren't completely honest with us, we can't sell you the merchandise.") Or how about Honda? ("No, madam, you cannot buy that car today. When you walked in here, you said you weren't buying today. We don't sell to liars, so you'll just have to come back tomorrow.") Come on. If we didn't sell to anyone who ever told a lie, we'd never sell anything. "Just looking...not buying today...just want a brochure..." do you blame them? Surely you don't think potential customers are going to walk in the door and offer the following: "Please help us. Here is our financial statement, here are our pay stubs for the past year, and this is what we expect to inherit in the next ten years. Now, why don't you tell us what you think we should buy? After all, you're the pro, you know what's best for us, so we'll do whatever you decide." Sorry, that will never happen. Better to expect potential customers to be on the defensive. They know what's in it for the salesperson—money, power, position and/or status. But what's in it for *them*? That's why, as salespeople, we have to learn to read between the lines, to be both straightforward and empathetic.

Since it's pointless to try to change any customer's personality and feelings, the real question is this: how do we sell the customer we're with? Liars, looky-lous, geeks—they all buy. Maybe not every customer is going to buy from us or even buy our products, but everyone buys, and the pros, the ones who sell the most, know that. Did you ever notice that no matter what the product—socks on hangers or multi-million dollar homes—some salespeople always seem to excel, consistently selling more than anyone else in their organization. In most of the golf course communities and businesses for which I do sales training, the number one—and sometimes also the number two—salesperson sells one hundred, two hundred, sometimes even three hundred percent more products or services than the rest of the sales staff.

What is this phenomenon? What the heck are those salespeople doing to sell so much more? Is it that they work much harder, putting in more hours than their associates? Nope. Do they kiss up to the boss—or become so friendly with the owner that they get all the good leads and customers? Again, nope. Maybe they know how to manipulate the facts and use emotional tie down? (You know, "Can't you just see your wife's face when you buy her that four carat ring? Make her happy, and think how much better your life will be. Don't worry about sending the kids to college; an asset like this is like money in the bank, and you can always borrow on it.") Or maybe it's just that old sales trick of a close-ended question: "Do you want the white dress or the red one, which will it be?" "Will afternoon or morning be better for you?" Do those salespeople simply shame their customers into buying? ("Everyone is driving a new car these days—well, that is, anyone who matters. Don't you want to make your family feel proud?") Or maybe it's the Ben Franklin Close. ("Don't think you want that lot? Well, let's just sit down and make a list. Put all the good things about living in this community on one side, and all the negative on the other. There. Now look at all those benefits—it's pretty clear to me. You should buy.") Or the Disney Close. This one is so goofy, pun intended, that I'm not even going to get into it.

So what's the trick? Well, get ready, because here, in one short sentence, you'll get your money's worth from this book: The trick is that there is no trick. There *is* a sales process, and that's what we're going to start talking about, a sales process that works. The one thing great salespeople have in common is that they don't use tricks. They are genuine, sincere. And these qualities cannot be faked. The leading salespeople in every field get their prospects to open up, they listen, and they make a heads-up presentation.

When great salespeople approach customers, they will, after the initial greeting, start getting their prospects to start talking about themselves. And if a prospect is allowed to do most of the talking, the salesperson will get more than enough information to make the sale. Most salespeople are so excited about what it is they're selling, and so self-centered, that they never give potential customers a chance to express what they need or want. They have no idea what any particular customer is really looking for. So how do you get prospects to tell you what's on their minds? Easy. You shut up and start listening. The best way to get people to start talking about themselves is to ask open-ended questions, ones that get the buyer to think. (Remember the six-second rule? The sound of the customer thinking?) The sound of the customer thinking is probably the rarest phenomenon in selling today.

Renee, one of the best salespeople I ever met, worked in a very exclusive golf course community in Palm Beach, Florida. I asked her what she did that helped her sell more than three times more than any other salesperson at her community. She said, "Craig, I have more then six billion ways of asking potential buyers what they would like to see happen today." It seemed to me that she might be exaggerating just a bit, but she then went on to explain. "Why six billion? Well, that's about how many people are on earth today, and we need to go about finding out how to reach each one of them in a different way. But essentially the question to the prospect is the same: what would you like to see happen today?" Renee is probably one of the best salespeople in the country, so her words are worth listening to. She told me she always started her conversation with a prospect with an open-ended question and followed it up with open commands. If the prospect pulled back and stopped talking, she encouraged him to continue ("that's interesting…tell me more" or "keep going"), and pretty soon she could sit back and watch the magic. Not only is getting a prospect to talk—and to keep going—a new experience for most salespeople; it's probably going to be a new experience for the potential customer as well. Rarely are customers treated in this way, so such a process separates the salesperson with this approach from competitors. And I shouldn't, at this point, have to tell you which approach works best.

You might give this idea a try the next time you're talking with a customer. Once she starts talking, letting down her guard and telling you what she likes, she will eventually let you know what she would like to see happen and how she processes information when making a decision about buying a product or service like the one you are selling. At this point your job becomes much, much easier. Asking open-ended questions will not only help you to understand your prospect; it will also allow you to gain empathy with her. Think of this process in terms of building a foundation. The first encounter with a customer enables you to gain the rapport, trust and respect you need in order to build something further: a long-term relationship. If three out of every four people asked say that trust is the number one reason they buy, and you want to sell more, what better and faster way to achieve that goal than to develop a genuine and equal relationship by encouraging customers to talk about themselves, not only taking the time to listen, but asking them to expand on what they say. Most potential buyers won't know what to say at first; they won't be able to remember the last time a salesperson treated them this way. So shut up. Let the silence—and the selling—begin.

This concept may take some getting used to. One of the favorite ways that prospects—consciously or unconsciously—throw most salespeople off in a direction contrary to shutting up and selling is that they actually attempt to sell the salesperson. A customer may say, "Mary, why don't you tell me a little about the advantages of the termite contract your company offers?" That's usually all it takes to get Mary to start dumping information all over the place. So look out. This is a trap, and most salespeople get caught in it. Let's say you are selling in a new home community and no prospects have come in for three days. Finally a couple arrives. After the usual greeting, Tom, the husband, says, "Well, John, tell me about this property. Why should Sally and I buy here?" After three lonely, boring days, chances are the moment you hear this question, you'll begin to babble. "Well, the prices are great, and the people who have bought into the community are all really terrific, and the builder we're using is amazing, state-of-the-art, only the finest quality materials, and everything is going to go up in value in the very near future, and…." Selling wholesale jewelry? Same rap, just some variations: "These are all original designs, and we always ship on time. Your customers will love these toe rings, and they have the best mark-up in the industry…." It doesn't take much intelligence to see that none of this talking does much to establish trust or rapport. The only hope for a salesperson in this position is that the customer might buy in spite of his sales skills, not because of them.

So back to our couple. Let's say Tom or Sally says to John, "We really want to be in a spacious community, and privacy is very important to us." Here we go again. Most salespeople, if they got this far, would immediately respond something like this: "Oh, yes, this would be an ideal place for you then. Our community is very spacious, very private." But there's a major problem here. To some people fifty feet between houses might seem just fine—but maybe Tom and Sally think spacious and/or private means being right in the middle of five acres. Who knows? You, the salesperson, certainly won't unless you can get a lot more information out of Tom and Sally. Privacy and spaciousness are in the eye of the beholder, the potential buyer. No salesperson has any way of really knowing what a prospect wants without asking for specific details.

The number one weapon I use on prospective clients is a discipline I have developed over the years: I call it the forty-five second presentation. Yes, that's all the time you need in the beginning to present your product or service to potential buyers. Give only a few facts, no puffery, and keep your comments to forty-five seconds. If they've asked about your product or services, they want only an opener, a glance at the menu. There's no need to give them the entire manual on your company at this point. If you keep it very short, you will give them something to launch their thoughts from, a way to begin the communication that is so lacking in the sales process today. Sure, we need to point out the benefits of whatever we're selling—but they have to be benefits to these *specific customers*, not to us or our friends or the last person who bought something from us. A benefit is worthy to be called one only if it is beneficial to a particular prospect.

Now, a lot of salespeople I speak to seem to think that in the eye of the prospect, a salesperson asking for more information or for a prospect's opinion about something is a sign of weakness. Nothing could be further from the truth. Let's say you go to the doctor and tell him you get headaches almost every day. Intense, painful headaches. You feel as though your whole brain is throbbing. And your doctor says, "Well, we'll just have to set you up for brain surgery tomorrow and fix that problem." Would you be satisfied with this response? Of course not—and no doctor worth his title would dismiss you and your needs in that way. He would instead ask more probing and open-ended questions: "When you say it's a throbbing pain, how does it usually start? Tell me more about it. Is it worse at any particular time of day or night? Is there anything that seems to help with the pain?" Then he might order some tests, maybe suggest that you get a second opinion, try some different treatments to find out the best way to minimize or eliminate the situation, always checking in with you for your reactions. He wouldn't try to sell you on surgery just because he needs the money to pay his daughter's tuition at Yale. At least I *hope* you don't have that kind of doctor.

And, to use our hypothetical doctor one more time, think of the term "bedside manner." Sympathy and understanding are qualities that one looks for in a good doctor. And they are qualities that a customer also appreciates in a sales professional, one who opens the door to a better than superficial relationship. Salespeople who are more consolatory than pushy are separating themselves from the pack and helping to overcome the horrible reputation that salespeople have given themselves. These people understand that making a commission cannot be their number one priority if they are going to compete successfully in today's sophisticated marketplace, and this will become increasingly true as more people in sales discover the techniques the top salespeople use to sell their products and services. The irony is that when a salesperson honestly puts the commission out of her mind for the moment and tries to find out what is best for a particular customer, rather than being overly persuasive, manipulative or pushy, she can then sit back and enjoy this new way of doing the job, make better commissions and have more fun in the process.

A quick review: Talk *with* your customers, not *at* them. Don't try to sell your potential customers; instead let them buy from you. Wouldn't you rather buy something than have it sold to you? "Hey, you're going to love this car, it's a great price, and think about all the fun you'll have driving it off-road." Not the safest thing to say to an unknown customer who may need four-wheel drive only because he lives on a road that is often slick and muddy. It's even possible that he believes most off-road vehicle drivers are damaging the earth's fragile ecosystem for their own selfish pleasure. Never presume to know a customer's idea of fun—or anything else about him, for that matter—after only a few minutes of conversation. Particularly if you've been doing all the talking.

A couple of months ago I went out to purchase a new SUV. I did my homework before I went. I looked up the exact SUV I wanted, a Montero Sport, XL with leather interior. I wanted white or gray, a light color. The last one I bought was black, and because a dirt road leads to my converted carriage house, my car always looks dirty. I also knew precisely how much money I was willing to part with to buy this new car. I walked into the dealership and asked to speak to the sales manager—the *real* sales manager, I added, since some dealerships call every salesperson a manager. I told the sales manager I knew exactly what I wanted to purchase, knew exactly what I was willing to pay, and didn't think it would be healthy either for me or for a salesperson to get together to discuss my purchase. I wanted to deal directly with the manager. This manager said he understood, but he asked if I would mind helping him by going with a rookie salesperson just so he could get a little practice. Well, being the kind-hearted person I am, and considering the fact that for most of my life I've made my living by selling, I said sure—but that the rookie had better watch out.

As I soon discovered, John, the salesperson, was a rookie only to this dealership. He'd actually been selling cars for years. He just wasn't as yet completely familiar with this particular line. The first thing out of his mouth was, "Welcome to Modesto Mitsubishi." Without giving me a chance to say a word, he went on to tell me what a smart and wonderful choice I had made in coming to look at their cars. I broke into his routine to let him know that I hadn't come to look, that I knew exactly what I wanted, and that I was there to buy. I thought I would be honest and approach with my dukes down, not up. I then told him exactly what I had told his manager. Without asking me another question, he hopped out of his chair—which, incidentally, was situated right in the middle of the showroom so everyone could hear our conversation—and started out to the lot. After we had passed nearly a hundred vehicles, he said, "Here they are. Just show me what you want." I pulled out the four-color printout I had taken from the internet, showing the exact SUV I wanted, including color, leather upholstery, and every other feature I was looking for, along with the dealer's cost. I handed it to him. He barely looked at it.

The first car he showed me was not the model I had requested. "Hey John," I said, "this is *not* what I want. I want the Sports Montero in the picture I gave you, the XL model with leather." He looked at the printout. "Oh," he said, and led me on a five-minute walk to another lot. "Here we are, the Montero Sport. Now, I can make a great deal on this one. It's last year's model, has only sixteen thousand miles on it." (He didn't add that it had probably also been well broken in by around twenty salesmen who had taken it home for a weekend since it had been sitting on the lot.) "We can give you a new warranty, and you'll save thousands from the price of a brand new one. I know it's not exactly the color you want" (it was red) "and it doesn't have a leather interior, but we can take it across the street and have the interior changed to leather and it will be better than new." *Wow, better than new. Now there's an interesting concept.* This guy clearly did not have a clue about me. At this point my dukes went up. "Hey John," I said, "I think this is the part where our discussion starts to get unhealthy. White or gray, Montero Sport, XL new, NOW! I'll find it in the lot and come and get you when I find it."

As you can probably imagine by now, the story goes on and on. Finally, after several more hours, I did drive home in my new SUV, but no thanks to my salesperson. To add insult to injury, his idea of a follow-up was to call me on my cell phone while I was on a break from giving a seminar in Reno. He wanted to ask me to give him good grades when the consulting company hired by his dealership called me to request an evaluation of the person who had sold me the car. *Thanks for the call, John; I'll be in touch if I ever meet anyone looking for a car who wants to deal with someone like you. In other words, never.*

How much easier it would have been if only John had taken the time right at the beginning to ask me exactly what I would like to see happen that day. Hell, he didn't even *need* to ask—I volunteered the information at the outset of our conversation. My search for a new car could have been this simple:

"Here's the printout, what do you have?"

"Let's see—Montero Sport XL with leather upholstery. Yes, we have one in gray."

"Fine, I'll take it."

End of story. Faster, more efficient sale. Some rapport and trust would have been established because the salesperson listened to find out what I wanted. Given that kind of treatment, I would probably have referred my friends to John.

Potential buyers have their dukes up because they haven't been listened to. Instead they've been talked *at* by a salesperson looking for a quick commission. Given the state of selling today, it's a great time to be in the business, because nothing could be easier than separating yourself from your competition just by making a few simple changes. The key is to get the prospect to open up. Encourage him to keep talking, clarify what you heard or ask for more explanation, and then let him know what you can or cannot do for him. When you talk, you must talk not about how great your product is or how happy it will make the buyer feel, but about the specific needs and wants of the buyer. It's that simple. Customers come with their dukes up. It's your job to get them to put their dukes down and open up. If you can do that, you're well on your way to selling significantly more with a lot less effort and have more fun doing it.

NOTES

4

NO PROOF, NO TALKING

o o o o o o o o o o o o o o o o o o o o o o o o o o o
Save the puffery for the car commercials.

When I give sales seminars, I tell salespeople that the one essential in establishing trust with a potential customer is to say only what they can prove. They don't actually have to *offer* proof every time they speak to a buyer, but what they say must be provable. If they follow this principle, their honesty and sincerity will come through in their presentation. More then 80% of communication takes place without words, and prospects pick up non-verbal signs fast when dealing with salespeople. Without fail, all the salespeople, managers and owners who attend my seminars agree that saying only what you can prove is more than important to gain trust during the sales process; it is *essential.* Who would argue with that? But it's obviously easier to talk about saying only what can be proved than it is to do it.

When I ask a salesperson to give me a presentation of a product, as if a potential buyer had just walked into her sales center or store and asked her about her product or service, this is what I generally hear:

Customer: "Well, Nancy, tell me a little more about this community."

Salesperson: "We have a really beautiful neighborhood here, really friendly people…."

Customer: *Wonder if I'll be harassed to attend boring block parties and carry on inane conversations about where everyone is from.*

Salesperson: "We have a world-class eighteen-hole championship golf course…."

Salesperson: *What constitutes "world class"?*

Salesperson: "The developer is great. We have award-winning house designs…."

Customer: *Who sponsors these awards? Are these the ones builders give themselves for being so clever?*

Salesperson: "The lots have awesome views…."

Customer: *In whose eyes?*

Salesperson: "Right now this development is one of the best values in the area; we're practically giving the property away. Prices are going up…."

C: *I wonder how much, and when. And if prices are going up, why are they pushing so hard to sell the property now?*

If this salesperson were really honest, she might add that she thinks the development is great because there's enough profit to pay the sales staff large commissions, cover all the overhead, and give the owner a big fat profit. *Caveat emptor.* No business is ever "practically giving away" their product.

Instead of using this vague and essentially dishonest approach, why not try the kind of presentation I ask attendees at my seminars to use to help establish rapport and trust fast, by saying only what can be proved to describe their product or services. It's called the snapshot presentation, also known as the forty-five second presentation we talked about earlier. Not only will it help to establish a good working relationship with your potential buyer, it will separate you from the competition—unless, of course, your competitors have also read this book and followed its advice. Just state the facts! Use bullet points. Let's try that initial interview again.

Customer: "Well, Nancy, tell me a little more about your community."

Salesperson: "Super Duper Community is a private, gated residential neighborhood with two swimming pools, three clubhouses, a snack bar, two restaurants, a lounge, a health spa, an equestrian center, jogging and walking trails, a recreational center with a card room, and a computer room. We can offer you either a home site or a new home."

That's it. Shut up, count to six, and let the potential buyer think. One...two...three...four...five...six. The next sound you will hear is the sound of the customer thinking—that rare moment in the sales process. But fortunately for you, you have given that time to the buyer and in doing so have gained the buyer's respect. Six seconds doesn't sound like much time, but for most salespeople it seems like an hour. So instead of granting this time to their potential customers, they fill up what should be a silent space with questions and unnecessary chit-chat.

Or they start firing off close-ended questions, the ones that require a *yes, no* or one-word answer, even if they've been taught that close-ended questions close the customer down. "Do you like the purple one or the blue one better?" What if the customer doesn't like either? There's no option being offered for that opinion, so in asking for an answer to a close-ended question, a salesperson is actually closing himself out of the presentation and preventing himself from doing his job, which is to find out what problems the customer might have with his product or service and then offer solutions to those problems. A customer may even close a salesperson out by answering with the response he thinks the salesperson wants to hear—before making a graceful exit and taking her business elsewhere, where she just might find someone who doesn't back her into a little closed area in which to respond to the product, but instead gives her the room to think for herself.

Hard as it may be the first few times you try this technique, just give a straight, honest presentation and let the silence begin. Count to six. If you talk or cover the silence with a close-ended question, you will lose all the work that went into your straightforward and honest presentation: the presentation that is different because it is designed to put the customer on the same level as you; the presentation that is different from the one used by most salespeople; the presentation designed to open up your prospects and get them to start talking about what it is they really want. If you will let them talk, they will tell you what they really want; they will also metaphorically hand you a map showing how to sell them. You may be able to solve a problem and make a sale—or you may have to end up with a no. But either way, this technique is going to save you time and make you a lot more money in the end.

Shutting potential customers off with close-ended questions or machine-gunning questions ("What would you like? A one bedroom? Two bedrooms? How many baths? One story? Two story?") is nothing but a nervous habit, a habit that comes from feeling uncomfortable and insecure with silence. Buyers can answer only one question at a time, so let them think. They're not going to get up and leave. "I'm sorry, but you haven't said anything for six seconds. We couldn't possibly buy anything from a salesperson who isn't constantly talking and telling us what to do. Let's go, Sylvia. We'll buy from someone who doesn't leave us time to think." Pretty unlikely scenario, isn't it?

It's our job as salespeople, selling in ever-increasingly sophisticated environments, to help open customers up, help them sort through their priorities so that we can find out what it is they really want. We need to get them to share their feeling and concerns. That's what it takes to be the best today, an empathetic approach. We have to understand our customers' side of things. When customers know we understand their side, their feelings about something, we are on our way to developing a real relationship—one based on trust, the core of the matter. After all, we are the pros. We deal with customers over and over again, hundreds of them a year, sometimes thousands. When we help potential buyers to solve problems, get them to open up—bingo. We have more sales, more buyers, more long-term relationships, more repeat business, more referrals—and, therefore, more money.

You can't start selling someone something until you know what that person wants. In fact, the potential customer may not even know himself what it is he is looking for. So help him find out. Remember, many customers will be wary, wanting to protect themselves emotionally from all the razzle-dazzle they've been through in other buying situations. And these are situations all of us who are selling have been through on one level or another with the hype of all the ads on TV, billboards, magazines, newspapers, the sides of buses, and now the internet—and I haven't even mentioned the visits to stores in search of goods or services. Of course customers have their guards up—that's a sure sign of a good potential customer, one smart enough to protect himself from all the phoniness.

If you let customers begin to talk, they will tell more than you need to know to make the sale. Can you buy that? Well, if you buy that and want to start making more sales, it behooves you to get customers to start talking—about themselves. After all, how hard can that be? And what better way to get people to start talking about themselves than by asking open-ended questions that make them think; questions that require thoughtful responses, not one-word answers that leave them feeling trapped; questions that give them room to feel comfortable enough to tell you what they really want.

My dad told me before I started out in my sales career that if I didn't understand what it was that a potential buyer was saying, it wasn't because I was stupid. It was just that the idea had not yet been communicated. He also told me not to start selling until I knew what it was the customer was interested in buying. Here's a good illustration of what he was talking about.

Customer: "We want a home with a great view."{

Salesperson: "Let's get in the car. Have I got a home for you! Incredible views—you can see forever, sixty or seventy miles into the desert from the back of the house, and the front looks right out into the golf course."

Now, does this salesperson really know what a great view is? Of course he does, right? Well, he knows what *he* thinks is a great view. But what does he know about his customers' definition? Maybe it's different from his. Let's try that scenario again.

Customer: "I want a home with a great view."

Salesperson: "A great view, okay. When you say 'a great view', what exactly do you mean?"

Customer: "Oh, you know—we want to look out our windows and see our yard and pool, nothing else. Just our pool, our landscaping, our stuff and nobody else's. And the last thing we want to look at is a damned golf course with a bunch of silly people wandering around spitting and cursing, trying to find their little balls."

In the first scenario the salesperson didn't have a clue as to what the customer wanted, so he made an assumption. And it is in making assumptions about prospective buyers that most salespeople are losing those potential buyers because they aren't listening. When the customers in the above scenario said they wanted a great view, that should have been just the beginning of the conversation, the first step in real communication. When a woman meets a man and says, "I just want a great relationship with someone else," the man doesn't respond—or at least I hope he doesn't—by saying, "Marry me and you will have a great relationship." That's a time for an open-ended question: "What, exactly, do you think makes a great relationship?" See? This stuff works, even at home. But back to the sale. Keep asking open-ended questions until you, as the professional salesperson, understand what it is the buyer is looking for. And repeat it back to the customer to make sure you understand. "Oh, so what you are saying is that a good view is one where you can see your pool and landscaping from all the rooms in your new home without having to look at the golf course at all." (One might wonder why a person with this particular definition of a great view is looking for a place in a golf resort, but stranger things have happened. Actually, many people who choose to live in golf resorts have no interest in the game.)

Simple rule: If it isn't true, don't say it! Now, how do you know when a view is awesome? Easy. When the *customer* says it's awesome. Then it's true in this particular situation—and when you call the view awesome, you are now using the word to compliment the customer, to show that you are listening to her needs and not your own. That same view can, in your humble opinion, be a horror once you are at home, relaxing in your favorite chair with a glass of wine after a productive day at work. But while you're with the customer, it's *awesome*.

You've probably been told that you have to believe in your product to sell it, that you've got to love it. Well, again, that's simply not true. What you have to believe is that the product you are selling is good for your *prospects*, your *potential buyers*. You have to believe that it solves something for them, fills a desire or need for *them*, not *you*. (I wonder if anyone has ever taken a survey of how many sellers of homes in golf resorts actually live in golf resorts themselves.) In any case, don't worry about the sale. Your job is simply to serve the customer and the sale will take care of itself.

This principle applies to sales of all kinds, even lunches in restaurants. Servers will do themselves a favor if they refrain from coming on with a scenario like this:

Server: "I'd really recommend this soup. You'll love it—it's my favorite. Believe me, you can't go wrong."

Customer: "What kind of soup is it?"

Salesperson: "Vegetable beef, the best aged Angus beef you can buy. It's absolutely the most delicious...."

Customer: "I'm a vegetarian...I'll pass. Just bring me a cup of coffee."

Guess it's best to try to know what the customer really wants, because even after a scenario like this one, the server is likely to follow up with a lot of hype about the desert menu, which isn't going to help at all. Chances are this customer will also turn out to be hypoglycemic. And while the loss of a sale may not mean much to a server, the loss of a good tip is another matter.

When I give sales seminars, I ask participants to call me down if they hear me say something they think I can't prove, and I do the same with them. It still amazes me how much empty chatter takes place, nothing but puffery, a bunch of stuff we can't prove. ("Look at this ring. Isn't it stunning? These rings are such a great deal, everybody loves them....")

When I ask salespeople what they answer when customers ask them if the property they are looking at is going to go up in value, 99.9 % of the time the salespeople say it's going up. They base this answer on the fact that the value of the property has gone up in the past. Or just on the idea that if customers think the price will go up, they'll buy, thinking they'll make money on the project. Going up? Prove it. The right answer to that question is, "I don't know." None of us can predict the future; there is no way we can assure anyone that a piece of property is going to go up in value. And if that would be your answer, you have passed the test, the trust test that every potential buyer gives a seller in one way or another. If you answer with what you think the customer wants to hear and not what's true, you're losing the game. Go for the gold; say only what you can prove. The customer has heard what someone has thought he wanted to hear before, almost always, in fact from every other salesperson he has spoken with. What he really wants to hear is the truth.

Sell the benefits—but *only* if they are benefits to the buyers. Your favorite food, style of house, model of car—all irrelevant. Sell customers what *they* want, not what you want to sell them—that is, if you want to sell more. I know it's hard to change old habits, but it helps to keep in mind the Golden Rule for Sales: *Do unto others as they would have done unto themselves.* A ring becomes stunning only when the customer says it is stunning. Say only what you can prove.

NOTES

5

SOLVE IT, IF YOU CAN

○ ○

Don't try to fix it. Leave that to the mechanics.

Inevitably, if you do your job as a salesperson correctly, you're going to hear objections and concerns from your potential buyers. And contrary to what you might think, specific objections to your product or service are actually good. They mean that the prospects like *almost* everything about what you are selling except for the few things they are bringing up. What they are really asking for is a way to solve the problems they have. And if there is no solution, only they can determine whether they see the problems as absolute deal killers or ones they can live with. It really doesn't matter if their objections have to do with price, terms, a perception, or a condition you can't change; objections can all be handled in much the same way. Unfortunately, the way most salespeople deal with their potential buyers' objections does not work. Salespeople usually try either to fix the problem or to ignore it. When a salesperson tries to fix a problem, he is, in effect, asking the customer to take an action to change something. And of course no problem goes away simply because it is ignored.

We need to *solve* problems for our customers whenever we have a solution to offer, but we cannot *fix* them. For example, if a prospect says, "We love the home, but we want a three-car garage, not a two-car garage," a good salesperson is not going to suggest that the prospect sell one of his cars. Nor is any competent jeweler going to suggest to a client who objects to a bracelet fitting too tightly that she lose some weight in order to make it fit. And if a person feels that 122 degrees in the summer is more heat than he can tolerate, the salesperson suggesting that it's a dry heat and that the customer will get used to it, is not doing much to help make the sale. Each of these examples is a *fix*; each one asks the potential buyer to make some change to eliminate the problem. An effective salesperson does not look for a fix, but rather for a *solution*. And if there is no solution, he will not ignore the issue; he will acknowledge it. Sometimes a customer raising an objection to a product or service will decide that she is able to live with the problem. Other times she may feel that the problem outweighs the advantages. Or she may simply want you to listen to her objections, to hear her out.

My wife, a personal fitness trainer, came home one night very upset. When I asked her what was wrong, she told me a man had been stalking her at the gym that day while she was doing her workout. "Really?" I said, then hit her with a barrage of questions: "What did you do? Did you tell the manager? Call the police? Confront the stalker? Ask someone for help? Do you want me to call the manager? Go after the stalker?" After I had received an increasingly exasperated "NO" to each of my questions, I finally asked her what she wanted me to do. "I don't want you to *do* anything," she said. "I just want you to listen. I don't want you to fix it; I just want to be heard."

Once you have really listened to what a customer has to say about your product or service, then you can start thinking about how to overcome whatever objections he has raised. And you, as a salesman, must learn to view those objections for what they are: an acceptance of *most* of the qualities your product or service is offering. The first important step in dealing with objections is to acknowledge them, no matter what they are. Most salespeople lose it right at this point; they try to fix the prospect's objection, or become defensive, or ignore the objection altogether. None of these approaches is productive. An effective salesperson will let the customer know she heard and understood what he said. The key word is *understood*. Once a salesperson acknowledges a concern, more than half of the time that concern immediately becomes a non-issue. This is such an important point that I'll say it again. *Acknowledge the objection your customer has raised, and more than half the time you will find that it will have no bearing on the outcome of the sale.* The irony of using this approach is that it's far easier on the salesperson than either trying to fix the situation or ignoring it. So acknowledge what the prospect tells you by isolating the issue and then repeating it back in your own words. Remember your body language. Be attentive, nod your head slightly in agreement, and keep good eye contact. Most of all, just listen, be yourself and be sincere.

Now let's look at a couple of Before (reading this book) and After (reading it and putting what you have learned into practice) scenarios:

BEFORE:

Bill: "We don't like the weather here."

Salesperson: "Actually, the winters here aren't so bad. It really doesn't snow all that much, and when it does, we do an excellent job of snow removal. As for the cold, well, your blood will thicken up soon and you'll get used to it."

AFTER:

Bill: "We don't like the weather here."

Salesperson: "When you say you don't like the weather here, Bill, can you tell me what you mean?" (Yes, this is an open-ended question.)

Bill: "Well, we know that most people who are thinking about buying here are concerned about the winters. That isn't our problem. We don't mind winter, but we hear the summers are a little on the cool side. We like to feel the seasons."

Salesperson: "So what I hear, Bill is that you and Mary would like to live in a place where the summers are nice and warm."

Mary: "That's right. Climate is pretty important to us. It could be the determining factor in whether or not we buy here."

Salesperson: "Tell me more about what you mean when you say you like warm summers." (This is an open command.)

Bill: "Oh, you know, summer days in the high seventies to the mid-eighties."

Salesperson: "Well, according to the U.S. weather service, our mean temperature during the summer months is 79.8 degrees. So when you purchase your home at Summer Ranch Estates, you can be assured of having the wonderful warm summer days you say are so important to you as well as all the other great things you said you liked about Summer Ranch."

Mary: "Well, that sounds fine. We thought it was cooler than that."

In the first scenario, you will see that the salesperson jumped to conclusions about the potential buyers' objection and did absolutely nothing to speak to it; instead, he simply told the potential buyers they would adjust to the climate. But in the second scenario, the salesperson wisely asked the potential buyers to be more specific about their concerns. And once he had pinned them down to exactly what they were looking for, it turned out that their objections were based on a misconception, and the property they were looking at was ideal for them. If you think the second scenario might involve a little more work in the sales process, consider which of these two techniques would more likely have led to a commission, a bonus, or even job retention.

Try to fix something, and people get their backs up. But if you acknowledge their objections and concerns and show

that you are empathetic toward them, your potential customers are probably going to live with that part of the product or service they object to. That's a fact; fifty-two percent
of all objections go away once they are acknowledged. People
seldom like *everything* about what they buy; they just have to
like *enough* of it to buy it. If a prospect says, "I don't like this
ring," make sure you understand what she means. Is she
looking for something in silver rather than gold? Is it the
price? The terms? Is it just too tight or too loose? Or does she
think it's really hideous?

Even when a client seems to have pinpointed a problem,
you may need more information. Suppose he says to you,
"Tom, we love everything about that house you showed us
but the price." Sounds simple enough. It's the money, right?
Wrong. Or at least possibly wrong. What about the price is
the objection? The size of the down payment? Or is it an
issue of value? Is the asking price too much in terms of the
current market? It might simply be that these people can't
afford this particular house—it's not in their budget or they
can't qualify for a loan. Could even be that for some reason
they don't quite trust either you or your company and the
issue of price is an emotional block. In any case, you can't
solve a problem until you know what it is. And how do you
find out? (Surely, you guessed this one correctly.) *Open-*

ended questions. Keep asking them until you find out *exactly* what the problem is. Don't assume anything. And don't try to fool the prospect into thinking you understand what he means, or the only person you're going to fool is yourself.

Once you have acknowledged the objection, it's time to go on to the next step: solve the problem or minimize it. Offer a solution—a different color, another size, or facts that speak to the customer's concern—*if you can.* For instance, let's say Mary, your potential buyer, who with Bill bought that piece of property in Summer View Ranch in the previous example (people buy more than one thing, you know), says she loves your jewelry, but she knows that silver tarnishes, and she doesn't want her fingers turning green or the jewelry looking dark and discolored unless it's polished frequently. The salesperson can solve this problem by explaining that all the silver jewelry in that line is Rhodium plated to keep it from tarnishing, a process approved by leading gemologists throughout the world, and assuring her that she won't end up with green fingers or tarnished rings. And he should then mention again the design and the price—the aspects of the jewelry she liked in the first place.

As you are trying to solve or minimize a problem, avoid the pitfall of suggesting a switch, that is, introducing another product instead of the one your prospect is interested in. Do that, and you're right back to the starting point; all the work that you've done thus far becomes useless. Consider this scenario:

Prospect: "I love this house. It has the perfect floor plan for me, it has tile floors instead of carpeting, the beamed ceilings are gorgeous, the fireplace is just the design I want, and the views are spectacular. There's only one problem—that vacant lot across the street. I don't really want to live with all the noise and mess of construction taking place."

Salesperson: "Well, how about that same floor plan in a different location? I have another model two blocks over where there are no vacant lots."

That suggestion might address one problem, but you can be sure that it will raise several others, and the prospect is likely to become confused and irritated by too much input. Instead the salesman at this point should use third party testimonials to minimize the problem, letting the prospect know that other people like her had expressed the same hesitation, but after moving in found that the problem was not as big an issue to them. He might suggest that the building of another house across the street might seem less important to her once she was in her new home, enjoying the views, the beams, the fireplace, the tile floors, and all the other aspects of the house she loved. In approaching the problem in this way, he still has the benefit of being able to build on all the work he has done thus far. If he has done his job, stressing all the advantages of the house she likes, chances are she will come to see that the construction process is only temporary and is not such a big issue to her.

If you can't offer your potential buyers a provable solution, then *don't*. Acknowledge the problem and then minimize it with third party testimonials, using PLT (People Like Themselves). Here's another scenario with Bill and Mary from Summer View Estates:

Mary: "There isn't a Nordstrom's for close to twenty-five miles from Summer View. I don't know, that's an awfully long drive…"

Salesperson: "Tell me more."

Bill: "Well, I don't care that much for myself; I play golf seven days a week and cards with the boys most evenings, but Mary likes to shop. She goes almost every day, and Nordstrom's is one of her favorite stores."

Salesperson: "So Mary, you would like to shop at Nordstrom's every day."

Mary: "Well, yes. They have great merchandise, and I have to be honest. Shopping with my girlfriends is a big part of my social life, and that might be too far to drive every day."

Salesperson: "I know of a few other women like you who have moved here from your area of the country and also liked shopping at Nordstrom's. They've said that after moving here to Summer View Ranch, the close proximity of a Nordstrom's was no longer such a big issue for them. Mary, when you purchase your home here, perhaps the distance to Nordstrom's won't be as big an issue for you. And you'll be able to enjoy all the aspects of Summer View Ranch that appeal to you—the close proximity to the clubhouse, the bridge nights, the clean country air, the style of the home you've been looking at, the price, and the view you thought was so great." [Note: Remember that this response must be provable. Use real third party testimonials. Don't go making up a 'fact' just to convince your potential buyer that you've solved the problem.]

This is how minimizing works. This salesperson didn't *solve* the problem. Nordstrom's is still twenty-three miles from Summer View Ranch. And he didn't *fix* the problem, either. He didn't suggest that Mary give up shopping and find something better to do with her time. He did suggest to Mary that *other people like her* were living at Summer View Ranch and enjoying life there *despite* the distance to the nearest Nordstrom's, so perhaps that would be the case for her as well.

Now you're ready for the final step, which you may already have noticed in this scenario: Repeat back to the prospect the benefits (as the prospect perceives them) of your product or service. The salesperson in the previous example mentioned each of the specific benefits of living in Summer View that had appealed to Mary. Let's go back to the jewelry for another example.

Salesperson: "So, Mary, when you buy this ring [here the salesperson is speaking to the potential buyer as though she were actually purchasing the product], you can be sure that your finger will not turn green. And besides not having to polish the ring, you'll have the price you wanted, the style you admired, and the rubies that mean so much to you."

Now when a potential buyer has an objection to your product or service, you won't have to shoot from the hip or give one of those all too obvious or defensive sales pitches that, unfortunately, most people in sales still resort to—despite the fact that they don't work very well. Now you have a tool to provide you with the necessary strategies to handle a prospect's objections, acknowledge them, either solve or minimize them, and finally speak to the prospect as though he were actually buying the product or service, emphasizing all the aspects that he likes and weighing them against the one or two objections. Here's a quick review:

Step 1: Acknowledge every problem or objection the customer raises, never ignoring any of them.

Step 2: Solve or minimize every problem; do not try to fix them.

Step 3: Speak of the customer as if he were a buyer, emphasizing the specific aspects of the product or service that he most likes about it. Repeat every benefit he has mentioned. Reminding him of what he liked about your product or service helps put things back in perspective.

Follow these steps, and your sales will improve.

NOTES

CONCLUSION

✦

SIX SECONDS TO YOUR NEXT SALE

Let's say you've done everything by the book—*this* book, that is. You've given the forty-five second presentation; you haven't dumped information; you've said nothing that you couldn't prove; you've asked open-ended questions; you've gotten your prospects to open up and do most of the talking; you've listened to their objections and acknowledged them, solving what you could and minimizing the rest. There's one more possible glitch you'll have to deal with, and you need to learn how to respond should it arise.

At the end of your appointment, your prospects may very well tell you they loved the property, enjoyed the tour, thought your presentation was excellent, best ever—but they have to think about it and will get back to you. At this point you may feel like saying, "You've got to be kidding me." But don't let your ego get overly involved here. The truth is, this is the most difficult moment in any sales process, the number one hurdle for salespeople no matter what they're selling.

It's possible that kind of response means that maybe your prospects *didn't* think your product was all that wonderful. After all, if they liked it as much as they told you they did, wouldn't they be buying?

The answer isn't simple. Perhaps they aren't buying because they still have an objection, a problem, some reason why they don't want to take the plunge, and they haven't chosen to tell you what that problem is. Why didn't they tell you? Maybe they aren't comfortable being that open with you. Maybe they don't even know themselves what is holding them back. Or maybe they have a policy of sleeping on every decision they make. In any case, it is our job as salespeople to try to find out why they aren't buying at the end of the appointment—and if there *is* an identifiable problem, try to solve it before they get away.

Participants in the seminars and workshops I present tell me that the statement "we want to think about it" is the one they hear most often after their sales presentations. When I ask these people how they respond to that statement, most of them seem baffled, try to say something clever, or come up with a canned answer. Here is an example of how the role-playing goes when I play the part of the prospect, giving some of the most typical responses of potential buyers, and the salespeople at the workshops play themselves:

Prospect: "We loved it, but we want to think about it. We'll give you a call."

Salesperson: "What do you have to think about?"

Prospect: "I don't know; we just need to talk it over and think about it some more."

Salesperson: "What do you mean by 'think about it.' You said you love it."

Prospect: "Well, yes, we do love it. But we aren't quite ready to sign yet."

Salesperson: "All right, you think about it and then give me a call."

Prospect: "Okay, we'll do that."

In this scenario, the salesperson has put everything into the hands of the prospect and will now be sitting around waiting for a call that may not come because now the prospect owns that phone call.

Here's another ineffective way of how to proceed:

Salesperson: "Think about it and I'll give you a call in a couple of days."

Prospect: "Fine."

Now the salesperson has simply delayed everything by two days. When he calls, chances are the prospects are going to say they're still thinking about it. Here the salesperson has made an assumption based on inadequate knowledge of the amount of time the prospects need to think.

And how about this approach:

Salesperson: "When do you think you'll be done thinking about it?"

Prospect: "I don't know. Can we think about that?

Is this conversation getting silly enough for you? If the prospects knew how much time they needed and wanted to tell the salesperson, they would have. And here's the worst one I ever heard, this from an old timeshare salesman who sold $700,000.00 homes in Hawaii. As he rolled a pen across the table toward his prospective buyers, he said, "Okay, why don't you take three minutes and think about it while I step out of the room. When I come back, you can tell me your answer." Wow, what technique! Imagine how effective a statement like that would be in pushing people looking to spend three quarters of a million dollars on a second home into making a quick decision.

So which of the above is the correct response to your prospects who say they want to think it over before signing? If you answered "none of the above," you would be right. All the remarks and questions the salespeople asked in these examples were close-ended, and they left the situation much the same as it was before anything was said. These approaches are more likely to close the door on a sale than help to complete it. What does one say at this time to keep the process moving? Well, there is *no right answer* to that one. It's different for every potential buyer, every time. But what the salesperson needs at this point is simple: *more information.*

What do people mean when they say they have to think about buying something? Maybe they still have some problem with the product that seems to them insurmountable, and maybe they are embarrassed or afraid to tell you about it. It's even possible that they've decided they don't like either you or your product. (And if so, that's okay—you won't waste time calling them back to ask what they're thinking when they have no intention of buying.) Some people simply feel it's polite to say they want to think about something. But a lot of others really do need some time before making a decision. They may be absolutely happy with your product or your presentation, but they still feel the need for some space, away from you, the salesperson, so they can talk in private. They may need to confer with their attorney or financial advisor, or check with a friend or relative. Whatever their reasons for asking for more time, though, you can be certain they exist. Don't be surprised if your potential buyers don't seem to know exactly what they need to think about.

That happens frequently. Just give them time to think. And any kind of high-pressure approach at this point is likely to drive them away, even if they are sincerely interested in what you are selling.

So what do you do at this point? I hope by now you've guessed it. That's right, ask an open-ended question, the same thing you did when your prospects first walked in the door of your store or community to keep their appointment. For example, "When you think about buying a home (or a line of jewelry) like this, what process do you go through?"

Prospects: "Well, actually, we haven't had a minute to ourselves since we got here and you showed us that home. We need to talk about it at dinner tonight and we'll get back to you."

Salesperson: "Great. Why don't we meet in the hotel lobby in the morning, say about 9:00 if that's good for you, and you can tell me how you feel, good or bad. How does that sound?"

Here the salesperson is showing respect for the prospects' privacy, their need to get some distance from the whole process of selling and consider, by themselves, what they want to do. Had the salesperson become pushy at this point, it's probable that he would have killed the sale right then. Here's another possibility:

Prospect: "I love your jewelry line, but my partner and I will have to think about it. I'll give you a call."

Salesperson: "John, when you think about buying a line of jewelry like this one, what procedure do you follow?"

Prospect: "Well, I always talk it over with my partner. We go over the numbers and then make a decision."

Salesperson: "I see. That sounds reasonable. Could I e-mail your partner a copy of our price list so that she can get a head start?"

Prospect: "Sure. That would be fine."

Salesperson: "Then I'll call you on, say, Tuesday, John, and see if you're interested in moving forward. Is that okay with you?"

Prospect. "Yes, Tuesday would be good. We'll talk then."

Both of these scenarios iilustrate the best follow-up tool for any product or service you sell: own the next contact. In the first it is the salesperson who proposed the time and place of the follow-up meeting. In the second it is the salesperson, not the prospect, who will be making the follow-up phone call. Even if a prospect says that she will call you in a week, you can still own the next contact if you suggest that if you haven't heard from her by the following Wednesday, you will call her. And it's also important to ask your prospect for her permission to call; in doing so you are allowing her to take part in the decision. Don't leave anything to hope or guesswork. When you own the next contact and have gotten permission from the prospect to make the next step, you are more likely to be on your way to a sale than you would be if you had left everything in the hands of your prospect.

Well, if you've read this far into this chapter, I think it's fair to assume you've at least skimmed the book up to here. The reading was the easy part. Now comes the hard part: doing what the book recommends. In the introduction we talked about change. If you really want to sell more and have more fun doing it, you have to change yourself. Remember the definition of insanity: the actions of someone who continues to perform the same routine over and over again expecting to get different results.

So what do you need to change? Probably everything about the way you make a sales presentation except your style. Your style is an important part of the sales process and is probably what brought you to this profession in the first place. Keep your basic style, but change the way you listen to potential clients and customers. Trust in a process that allows you to talk with your prospects and find out what their real interests are. Using the forty-five second presentation, get your prospects to talk first about themselves and their perceptions and desires. Ask open-ended questions to discover the specifics of these perceptions and desires, and continue with your questions until both you and the prospects have a clear understanding of their agendas. Then show, demonstrate and talk about *only* those aspects of your product or service that are pertinent to these prospects' needs and desires.

Don't forget to review and evaluate all you have demonstrated, shown and talked about with your potential buyers. Acknowledge every objection or problem. Offer solutions, but don't try to fix your prospects' concerns. Solve or minimize them, remembering to use third party testimonials where appropriate, and talk with your prospects as though they were buyers. Leave *your* agenda—as well as that of your boss and the other people in your organization—out of the sales process. And, most importantly, as you ask those essential open-ended questions that will give you all the information you need to work effectively with your prospects, don't forget to shut up and count slowly to six, giving the prospects time to think about answers. Do this, and you just might be six seconds away from your next sale. In fact, do all of this, and you will have earned the right to *ask* for the sale.

Now it's all up to you. Happy shutting up and selling.

NOTES

NOTES

NOTES

NOTES

0-595-27517-6

Printed in the United States
32345LVS00003B/136-264

9 780595 275175